Abraham

James Poole

ISBN: 978-1-78364-456-8

The Open Bible Trust
Fordland Mount, Upper Basildon,
Reading, RG8 8LU, UK.

www.obt.org.uk

("CV" is the Concordant Version, "RAV" is the Revised Authorised Version.)

Abraham

Contents

Introduction

Some of us may remember our Sunday School days, when we were taught, and rightly so, that Abraham is the greatest example of faith in the Old Testament. He did not merely believe *in* God, for demons do that and fear and tremble (James 2:19), but he acted on his belief.

We are foolish if we do not believe in the existence of God.

> "For the invisible things of Him from the creation of the world are clearly seen, being understood by the things that are made, even His eternal power and Godhead (Deity); so that they (and *we* also) are without excuse" (Romans 1:20).

Abraham, originally named Abram, believed God when God spoke to him and revealed some gracious promises to him and he left his country, Ur of the Chaldeans, his relations and his father's house, to go to a land which God would show him

(Genesis 12:1-4). That is the essence of true faith. It is followed by obedience.

James Poole

The call of Abram

After his father's death Abram departed from Haran with his wife, but also took his nephew Lot, as well all his possessions and the souls born to him in Haran; and they came to the land of Canaan (Genesis 12:5).

What a devastating command God had given!

> "Get thee out" (Genesis 12:1),

but faith laid hold of God's gracious promises. Forsaking everything connected with Ur of the Chaldeans, a highly civilised but idolatrous country, Abram went out, not knowing whither he was going. Putting his hand in the hand of God, he was led safely into the land of Canaan.

Do we, members of Christ's body, lay hold by faith upon our heavenly expectation in Christ Jesus, where our future blessings lie in the heavenly realms, just as Abram believed God's earthly promises in Christ? Imitating Abram should prevent us from being conformed to this present evil age, as we, like Abram, forsake its seductive attractions (Colossians 3:1-4 CV).

In the Promised Land

On entering the land of Canaan, Abram found himself face to face with the warlike Canaanites, who held the land by right of conquest. Abram had been promised the land by God, and only faith in that promise will support him in the presence of the Canaanites. To strengthen his faith, God appeared to him a second time, saying,

> "Unto thy seed will I give this land" (Genesis 12:7).

His faith strengthened, Abram built an altar, pitched his tent, and called upon the name Jehovah. The altar marked his covenant relationship with God; the tent expressed his claims to that relationship (separation from the ungodly Canaanites); and the calling on the name of Jehovah showed his reliance on Him for protection and sustenance.

Abram's tent was pitched on a mountain, from where he could view two cities, Ai, meaning "a heap", and Bethel, "the house of God". His gaze was toward Bethel, "the house of God", as that time occupied by the Canaanites' gods. Abram

> "looked for a city which hath foundations whose builder and maker is God" (Hebrews 11:10),

the New Jerusalem (Revelation 21:2).

Backsliding

Canaan was struck by a famine and Abram's faith wavered. Instead of trusting in God to provide him with sustenance, he journeyed down to Egypt where there was wheat. Note that it is always *down* into Egypt, never *up*!

Sarai, Abram's wife, was a beautiful woman and Abram feared that Pharaoh, king of Egypt, might seduce her and kill him. So he passed her off as his sister (a half truth).

> "Oh, what a tangled web we weave, when first we practise to deceive!"

Pharaoh did take Sarai into his house and treated Abram well for her sake, supplying him with many cattle, menservants, and maidservants (Genesis 12:10-16). But gone was the altar; gone was the tent; and gone was calling on the name of Jehovah. Abram became a servile courtier in the house of Pharaoh. This was Satan's attempt to destroy the promised seed through Sarai.

Abram was helpless and could have been lost, but for the ever-faithful God, Who came to the rescue. God's promise and honour were at stake, so He plagued Pharaoh and his household, disclosing to him that Sarai was Abram's wife. Pharaoh was furious. He had been misled by Abram, and he sent both Abram and Sarai packing, with all their possessions, back to Canaan, back to the altar, back to the tent, and back for a renewal of communion and fellowship with Jehovah (Genesis 12:17-20).

Backsliding often brings with it scars of the lapse from the pathway of faith. The wealth that Abram brought out of Egypt later on proved a source of vexation. The cattle estranged him from Lot, and an Egyptian maid, Hagar, became the cause of much distress.

Choices

When it came to the parting of the way, Abram wisely gave Lot first choice of which part of the land to dwell in. Lot lifted up his *own* eyes and made his *own* choice: the plains of Jordan were

> "well watered everywhere, before the Lord destroyed Sodom and Gomorrah, even as the garden of the Lord."

He dwelt in one of the cities of the plain and pitched his tent toward Sodom.

> "But the men of Sodom were wicked and sinners before the Lord exceedingly" (Genesis 13:10-13).

God then said to Abram,

> "Lift up now thine eyes, and look from the place where thou art, northward, southward, eastward, and westward, for all the land which thou seest, to thee will I give it, and to

> thy seed forever. And I will make thy seed as the dust of the earth; so that, if a man can number the dust of the earth, then shall thy seed also be numbered. Arise walk through the land in the length of it and in the breadth of it; for I will give it unto thee" (Genesis 13:14-17).

Such amplification of God's promise was a further strengthening of Abram's faith.

The soldier

We have seen a pilgrim with a tent and an altar; now we shall see a soldier fighting against kings. The new departure in life is the direct fruit of Abram's restoration, walking in steady fellowship with the Lord. Abram, with 319 trained servants, defeats an army of four kings: Amraphel, king of Shinar; Arioch, king of Ellasar; Chedorlaomer, king of Elam; and Tidal, king of Goim. These had already defeated Bera, King of Sodom; Birsha, king of Gomorrah; Shinab, king of Admah; Shemeber, king of Zeboiim; and the king of Bela (that is Zoar).

Abram rescued Lot, his nephew, who had been captured, and all his goods. He liberated the prisoners of war and returned laden with spoils. This Abram did in the power of the Lord, who delivered his enemies into his hand. Furthermore, he would not take any of the spoils for himself, for he had come to rely on the Lord, the Most High God, the Possessor of heaven and earth, Who had supplied all his needs and continued to do so.

We now come to a fleeting figure in history, Melchizedek, the king of Salem (later Jerusalem) who was also the priest of the Most High God. He brought out bread and wine, symbols of sacrifice, and Abram gave tithes of all he possessed to him. Melchizedek is a type of Christ, the Great High Priest (Genesis 14:1-24).

Since the Aaronic priesthood in Levi was descended from Abram, Abram was, in effect, paying tithes to Melchizedek as a type of Christ. This fact should have been indisputable proof to Israel that the priesthood of Christ is superior to that of Aaron (Hebrew 7:9-11).

We, who are in Christ and who are soldiers in our own day and age, do not fight against human kings but against the principalities and powers, the rulers of the darkness of this age. They do all they can to prevent us from enjoying, by faith, our inheritance in Christ Jesus in the heavenly realms. They resent our intrusion there. But we are provided with heavenly armour to protect us. This is the panoply of God, provided for us in

Ephesians 6:10-17: the girdle of truth; the breastplate of righteousness; the sandals of peace; the large shield of faith; the helmet of salvation; and the sword of the spirit, the Word of God, our only offensive weapon. These five pieces of armour completely protect us. They are all attributes of Christ our Lord. He is our heavenly armour, and we are exhorted to put Him on with prayer.

The attack of our foes in the heavenly places cannot rob us of our membership of the Body of Christ. That is outside all possible robbery. The attack is against the enjoyment of our possessions in Christ Jesus and the possibility of the loss of a reward for faithfulness (1 Corinthians 3:11-15; 2 Timothy 4:7-8).

Two dangers menaced Abram in the capacity of a soldier; fear of death and love of gain. So Jehovah fortifies Abram against these perils by further grants of grace.

"Fear not, Abram; I am thy shield and thy exceeding great reward" (Genesis 15:1; cf, our shield in Ephesians 6:16).

Abram's justifying faith

We now come to that well known verse in Genesis 15:6, where it is said that Abram "believed in the Lord, and He *counted it to him for righteousness*". Paul quotes this verse in his epistle to the Romans, 4:3. Paul insists upon sheer unadulterated faith in Christ's death and resurrection; that faith justifies a believer before God (Romans 4:4-5).

Where do good works come in? The two sides, faith and works, are clearly stated in Ephesians 2:8-10.

> "For by grace are ye saved through faith; and that not of yourselves; it is the gift of God, not of works, lest any man should boast, for we are His workmanship (achievement CV), created in Christ Jesus unto good works, which God hath before ordained (prepared) that we should walk in them."

Paul also insists

> "that those who have believed might be careful to maintain good works" (Titus 3:8, RAV).

But this justifying faith of Abram, regarding God's promise of the multitude of his descendants "as the stars of heaven", was to be tested.

Another lapse of faith

The promise of an heir called for a fresh exercise of faith on Abram's and Sarai's part. Sarai was barren. Both were advanced in age, and it was contrary to nature for a child to be born to them. They both felt their impotence. Conscious of their inability, Abram and Sarai decided upon a plan that seemed to make possible the advent of an heir.

Sarai took Hagar, her Egyptian bond maid, and gave her to Abram to be his wife (Genesis 16:1-3, 15). This was in accordance with the existing laws before Sinai, known as the laws of Khammurabi.

The child born of that union was Ishmael,

> "A wild ass among men; his hand will be against every man and every man's hand against him" (RAV).

He was debarred from the inheritance, and Abram was eventually ordered to cast him out (Genesis 16:12; 21:10). However, God did take pity on

Ishmael and made of him the father of a great nation (the Arabs, Genesis 17:20).

The Hagar scheme originated in self occupation and distrust of God's word. The flesh in us makes it hard sometimes to have faith in God's power.

El-Shaddai

Some fifteen years later, when Abram was ninety-nine years old, the Lord appeared to him and said (to him),

> "I am *El-Shaddai*; walk before me and be thou perfect" (not sinless, but with whole-hearted trust in the Lord) (Genesis 17:1).

I am *El-Shaddai*, the One able to perform His promise, the One whose might is irresistible.

Abram sees God in a new light. With this new conception of God, comes a new outlook upon life and a new attitude toward God. God makes Himself known by a new name, and Abram receives a new name, Abraham – father of many nations (Genesis 17:1-5).

The flesh, which limited God's power and leaned on its own contrivances, is put off. Abraham is ordered to circumcise himself, and his flesh becomes the mark and seal of Jehovah's victory (Genesis 17:24).

Justification by faith

It is here that I am going to bring in Romans 4:17-25, which seems appropriate at this point.

> "As it is written, 'I have made thee a father of many nations', before Him Whom he believed, even God, Who quickeneth the dead and calleth those things which be not as though they were, who against hope believed in hope, that he might become the father of many nations, according to that which was spoken, 'So shall thy seed bc'. And being not weak in faith, he considered not his body, now dead, when he was about an hundred years old, neither yet the deadness of Sarah's womb. He staggered not at the promise of God, through unbelief, but was strong in faith, giving glory to God; and being fully persuaded that, what He had promised, He was able also to perform. And therefore it was imputed to him for righteousness."

> "Now it was not written for his sake alone that it was imputed to him, but for us also, to whom it shall be imputed, if we believe on Him that raised up Jesus our Lord from the dead, Who was delivered up for our offences and was raised again for our justification."

Thus, we, too, are justified by the simple process of believing God, What could be simpler than to believe God's testimony concerning His Son, and to trust in Him as our Saviour and Lord?

Faith has not the least merit. We do not deem it meritorious to believe an honest man (let alone God). Faith requires no effort. It is not work. It is the simplest, easiest, and freest channel God could choose to convey His righteousness to us. Let us praise Him that salvation is through faith that it may accord with grace.

The intercessor

Shortly after this, the Lord appeared to Abraham under the oaks of Mamre and renewed His promise of an heir to Abraham. Before departing the Lord confided in Abraham concerning Sodom's awful doom.

We now see Abraham cast in another role, that of an intercessor pleading before the Judge of all the earth, on behalf of the guilty cities of the plain. Abraham knew of Lot's sojourn in Sodom. He knew too that Lot's influence for God there was very feeble at the best, so perhaps he endeavoured to supply by prayer the deficiency of a testimony marred by worldliness and inconsistency.

Abraham persistently pleaded with God to spare the city, if only ten righteous men could be found there. But that number, having been scaled down from fifty, was not there. Lot and his daughters were rescued, but his wife looked back and became a pillar of salt. Thus, Sodom was destroyed (Genesis 19:10-11, 23-29).

When we pray for unbelieving relatives and friends, we should be very humble in our approach to God. God's grace is sovereign, and He does the choosing of His elect in this dispensation of grace. But do not stop praying for *all* mankind, for we do not know whom God has chosen.

Repetition of a previous lapse of faith

After these things Abraham went to Gerar and for the fear of a man, Abimelech, King of Gerar, he employed the same tactics as he had done in Egypt. He again passed off Sarah as his sister. But God intervened again and rescued Abraham. Abimelech naturally felt aggrieved that he had been deceived by Abraham and might have died if God had not told him the truth in a dream (Genesis 20:1-18). Who would have thought that Abraham would have been caught in the same trap twice?

The lesson that I learn from this is that however advanced I may be in the knowledge of God, however mature I may grow in God's grace, then is the time to walk humbly with God, for Satan never ceases to try to catch us out and cause us to stumble.

> "Let him that thinketh he standeth take heed lest he fall" (1Corinthians 10:12).

Deflections from God's path expose us to Satan's attacks, and he is ever on the alert to take advantage of opportunities and use them to the best of his ability.

Yet Satan is but an agent in carrying out God's disciplinary plans (Job 2:6-7). When we fall into Satan's hands and experience his evil designs, it is only for the purpose of God to lead us back to a closer walk with Him.

Satan's malignity and the blessed results which the wisdom of God accomplishes through him remind me of the story of an artist who, through jealousy, flung a sponge at the canvas of a rival, intending to spoil his work. But he produced by the merest accident the very effect which the fellow artist's utmost efforts had failed to do. God's purposes are at times obscure, but in His sovereignty He produces good out of evil.

Laughs

There are two laughs recorded in Genesis; Sarah's (18:11-15) and Abraham's (17:17). Sarah's laugh was one of *unbelief* and she was rebuked by the Lord. Abraham's laugh was the laugh of *faith*, for he bowed himself before the Lord as he laughed. Moreover, Abraham's plea to the Lord that Ishmael "might live before God" (Genesis 17:18) was not in unbelief of the promise in Isaac, but was in compassion for Ishmael's welfare (Genesis 17:20-21).

Isaac is born

At last Isaac is born. Oh, the joy that must have welled up in the hearts of Abraham and Sarah! The ever faithful Jehovah had fulfilled His promise at last. In Isaac, and his descendants to follow, lay all the wondrous promises of God to Abraham and all the families of the earth, through Christ foremost of all, the promised seed through Whom all blessings flow, both earthly and heavenly. The Hebrew word for Isaac means "laughter" (Genesis 21:1-8). We may also laugh at our foes, in the grace and power of our heavenly Father, through our Lord Jesus Christ.

We would, perhaps, think that the narrative of Abraham would end here, at the arrival of the promised seed, Isaac. But there lay a further test for Abraham's faith, the greatest test of his life.

Summary of Abraham's faith so far

Before we study Abraham's supreme act of faith, it would be profitable to go back over his life and watch his faith grow from the moment of its inception. God promised Abram that from him a great nation, Israel, would descend. His name would be great and a blessing to all the families of the earth. No further details are given. God waited for his response to leave Ur of the Chaldeans and be led into a land that God was to show him.

There was partial obedience of faith when Abram, accompanied by his father Terah, went as far as Haran. When his father died there, Abram was free to fully obey God's call, but he took Lot.

On arriving in the land of Canaan, Abram is confronted with the Canaanite hosts. God strengthens his faith by a promise to give the land to his seed;

"And to thy seed will I give this land".

Thus strengthened, Abram enters into worship and communion with God. His faith grows stronger when, from a mountain top, he views two cities, Ai (a heap), and Bethel (the house of God), then occupied by the gods of Canaan. But he looked for a city with foundations built by God, the New Jerusalem (Revelation21:2).

At this point of faith, there is a lapse, caused by a famine in the land, and, forsaking his trust in God, Abram descends into Egypt. In Egypt Abram is helpless, and God takes the initiative and rescues him. He is restored to fellowship with God, a sadder yet wiser man.

After the parting of the ways from nephew Lot, Abram is contented to rest on God's choice of the land and on His providence. God applied His promise by disclosing the boundaries of the land, north, south, east, and west, as far as the horizons. He also told Abram that His descendants would be likened to the dust of the earth for multitude. This was a further strengthening of Abram's faith.

Now strong in faith, Abram defeats a mighty king, Chedorlaomer and his allies. He rescues Lot and refuses to take the spoils of conquest for sustenance, for Abram's faith now rests in the Most High God, Possessor of heaven and earth.

> "Fear not, Abram: I am thy shield and thy exceeding great reward" (Genesis 15:1)

was said by God to Abram to allay his fears of death in possible future conflicts and to encourage him to continue to trust in God's providence.

So strong now is Abram's faith that he believes God's promise of his descendants being as numerous as the stars in heaven for multitude. The previous promise of the dust of the earth suggests *natural* descendants, while the stars of heaven suggest *spiritual* descendants. Abram's faith in this latter promise is counted to him for righteousness. Abram and Sarai were both getting on in years, and lack of faith in God's promise of a son caused them to attempt to gain an heir to the promise by Hagar, Sarai's Egyptian maid-servant. This was not acceptable to God, and Ishmael, the son of this union, was eventually cast out.

The revelation of God to Abram in His title of *El-Shaddai* – the One able to perform His promises, Whose might is irresistible – and the command to walk before God and be perfect (whole-hearted), again strengthen his faith. A new name is given to Abram. Now he is Abraham, father of many nations.

There was one further bad lapse of faith, when Abraham feared Abimelech, King of Gerar, and again passed off Sarah as his sister, just as he had done to Pharaoh, King of Egypt, some years earlier. Again God rescued Abraham in similar circumstances. In spite of this lapse, Abraham grew stronger and stronger in faith, fully persuaded that God would keep His promise of an heir to him and Sarah.

Surely the testing of Abraham's faith, progressively, is a classic example of how God deals with *us*, that He never tests us above what we are able to bear, but with the test provides us not with a way of escape from the test but a blessed sequel to follow (1 Corinthians 10:13).

Abraham's faith in God, after many testings, had become stabilised in process of time. But there was one more test to come, the greatest monument of his faith.

The supreme test of Abraham's faith

One day God said to Abraham, "Take now thy son, thine only son whom thou lovest, even Isaac, and get thee into the land of Moriah; and offer him there for a burnt offering, upon one of the mountains which I will tell thee of" (Genesis 22:2). What were Abraham's feelings at such a command,

> "Thine only son whom thou lovest."?

It was like rubbing salt in an open wound. Yet Abraham's faith overcame his feelings. He did not delay in obedience, He

> "rose up early in the morning and saddled his ass and took two of his young men with him and Isaac his son and cut the wood for the burnt offering and rose up and went to the place of which God had told him" (Genesis 22:3).

When the appointed place was reached, Abraham told the two young men to

> "abide with the ass, and I and the lad will go yonder and worship and come again to you" (Genesis 22:5).

Abraham had not the remotest idea how God could deliver Isaac, but he knew that all God's promises were bound up in his son, and that God, the Almighty, was able to raise him from the dead (Hebrews 11:19).

But a much sterner test lay ahead. As the two advanced toward the mountain, Isaac said to his father,

> "Behold the fire and the wood, but where is the lamb for the burnt offering?" (v7).

Could Abraham say to the son of his love,

> "You are the burnt offering, my son?"

How gloriously Abraham's faith rose above the knife thrust at his heart! His answer was,

> "God will provide Himself a lamb for a burnt offering, my son" (v8).

The climax of Abraham's faith had arrived. He built the altar, laid the wood in order, and bound Isaac, his son, upon the altar, upon the wood.

> "And Abraham stretched forth his hand and took the knife to slay his son" (vs. 9-10).

It was then that the angel of the Lord intervened, saying,

> "Lay not thine hand upon the lad, neither do thou anything unto him; for now I know that thou fearest God, seeing thou hast not withheld thy son, thine only son, from Me" (v 12).

> "And Abraham lifted up his eyes and looked, and behold behind him, a ram caught

> in a thicket by his horns; and Abraham went and took the ram and offered him up for a burnt offering in the stead of his son, and Abraham called the name of the place Jehovah-Jireh, 'the Lord will provide'" (vs. 13-14).

And God, because of Abraham's obedient faith in not withholding his son, his only son, Isaac, reiterated His promises with an oath, making them absolutely unconditional, inviolate, regardless of whatever lay ahead in the future, regardless of the way the nation of Israel behaved, for all depended upon God's faithfulness (vs. 16-18).

We have now come to the end of Abraham. He died in a good old age (175 years old), surrounded by many possessions and sons and daughters, by his second wife, Keturah (Genesis 25:1-4, 7, 8).

The antitype

Thousands of years later another Father went hand in hand with His Son to sacrifice Him. The Father was God Himself; the Son, His only begotten, beloved Son, our Lord Jesus Christ. This time there was no substitute, no ram caught in a thicket, to offer up instead of His Son. This was the Lamb of God that takes away the sin of the world (John 1:29). The ram caught in the thicket was an *unwilling* sacrifice, in contrast to the Lamb of God Who was a *willing* sacrifice on our behalf. Christ *willingly* obeyed His Father's will in His precious redeeming love.

Having looked at Abraham, we hope that our dull hearts and minds may have a better understanding of what God the Father went through as His Son approached Calvary. We pray that we may also appreciate more the sufferings of His Son, the excruciating physical pain of crucifixion, the abuse and insults of the soldiers and the crowd, and the mocking cry of the chief priests; "He saved others' Himself He cannot save". How ironically true this statement is, for if He had saved Himself, none of us would now be saved (Matthew 27:41-42).

> "My God, My God, why hast Thou forsaken Me?"

was His agonised cry (Matthew 27:46). He was abandoned by His Father and no substitute provided, because He was the only One good enough to pay the price of sin, and this Son "was made sin for us" (not merely a sin offering for the word 'offering' does not occur in the Greek).

> "He who knew no sin, that we might be made the righteousness of God, in Him" (2Corinthians 5:21 RAV).

Did the Creator of the heavens and earth, the Almighty, all-powerful One, have no feelings when His Son was crucified? It is almost blasphemy to ask such a question! God the Father *did* suffer. Abraham, the friend of God, in his personal sufferings in his heart as he prepared to sacrifice his son, was permitted in a measure to portray something of God the Father's sufferings when He offered up His dearly beloved Son, our Lord and Saviour.

I always feel that in contemplating God the Father's sufferings, we are on holy ground. Does not this call for a presentation of ourselves and bodies to God, a living sacrifice, holy, acceptable unto God, which is, after all, only our reasonable service?

Paul does not order us to do this. He *beseeches* us, by the mercies of God which we have received (Romans 12:1), to give Him our bodies as well as our hearts and minds.

More on Abraham

Abraham and his seed

By William Henry, Michael Penny and Sylvia Penny

In Genesis 12, we read of God's covenant promise to Abraham to make him a great nation, to bless him and to bless all people on earth through him. As we progress through Genesis, this covenant was confirmed with Abraham and with his immediate seed, Isaac and Jacob. Later, further promises were made to his subsequent seed, the Twelve Tribes of Israel.

How were these promises to be implemented as the seed of Abraham grew into a nation - a nation that largely failed to follow the Lord faithfully as their father Abraham had done? What does the rest of the Old Testament have to say about the seed of Abraham? Was there any change in the New Testament? Where do those who are not the physical seed of Abraham (i.e. Gentiles) fit into all this?

This book traces the Lord's dealings with Abraham and his seed throughout the Old and New Testaments and considers whether God is still dealing with the seed of Abraham today.

Portraits of the Patriarchs

By William Henry, Andrew Marple, Michael Penny and Sylvia Penny

Portraits of the Patriarchs is based on Abraham, Isaac, Jacob and Joseph.

The four authors do an excellent job of not only bringing before us the important issues in the lives of the four patriarchs (i.e. lessons in history).

However, they also, in considering the lives and experiences of Abraham, Isaac, Jacob and Joseph, draw out lessons of faith and practice which are applicable to 21st century Christians.

Abraham's Progress in the Covenants of God

By Glen Burch

This publication commences with an explanation of covenants in general, before turning to the specific covenants that God made with Abraham, which are dealt with and covered well. However, the main theme is Abraham's progress in those covenants.

In the preface the author introduces Abraham's life as a pattern that can help Christian's today, and this theme is developed and continues throughout the booklet. In Abraham, then, we find an example of faith that should attract and motivate every Christian.

This booklet will be a blessing to all Christians, especially those who are new to the faith or new to reading the Bible.

By Faith Abraham

By W M Henry

Hebrews chapter 11 records that by faith Abraham when called went, even though he did not know where he was going! By faith Abraham made his home in the Promised Land like a stranger! By faith Abraham, even though he was past age, became a father! By faith Abraham, when tested, offered up Isaac.

William Henry considers each of these with references back to Genesis, giving much helpful background. He concludes the booklet with doctrinal and practical applications both of which are pertinent and relevant to everyone today.

****

Please note:

Further details of all the books here can be seen on **www.obt.org.uk**

The can be ordered from the website and also from

The Open Bible Trust,
Fordland Mount, Upper Basildon,
Reading, RG8 8LU, UK.

They are also available as eBooks from Amazon and Apple, and also as KDP paperbacks from Amazon.

Free sample

For a free sample of
the Open Bible Trust's magazine *Search*,
please email

admin@obt.org.uk

or visit

www.obt.org.uk/search

About the author

James Poole was born in Finchley, London, in 1909 and took a course in Business Training at the City of London College. During his working years he was employed by various institutions and banks in the City of London. When he wrote this booklet he was enjoying retirement with his wife in Eastbourne, Sussex, but has since fallen asleep in Christ.

Also by James Poole

Further details of all the books here can be seen on **www.obt.org.uk**

The can be ordered from the website and also from

The Open Bible Trust,
Fordland Mount, Upper Basildon,
Reading, RG8 8LU, UK.

They are also available as eBooks from Amazon and Apple, and also as KDP paperbacks from Amazon.

About this book

Abraham

The author takes the read through the life of Abraham. Starting with the call by God, James Poole follows Abraham from Ur of the Chaldees, to Haran, into the Promised Land, onto Egypt and then back to Canaan.

But as well as the geographic journey he also put before the readers the journey of Abraham faith; his justifying faith when he believed God who then considered Abraham righteous. However, as we continue with Abraham we see lapses in his trust of God, but in the end we find a man who has such faith in God that he was willing to sacrifice Isaac, his only son, because he was so convinced that God would have to raise Isaac from the dead if God was to keep his promises.

Publications of The Open Bible Trust must be in accordance with its evangelical, fundamental and dispensational basis. However, beyond this minimum, writers are free to express whatever beliefs they may have as their own understanding, provided that the aim in so doing is to further the object of The Open Bible Trust. A copy of the doctrinal basis is available at

www.obt.org.uk/doctrinal-basis

or from:

THE OPEN BIBLE TRUST
Fordland Mount, Upper Basildon,
Reading, RG8 8LU, GB

www.ingramcontent.com/pod-product-compliance
Lightning Source LLC
LaVergne TN
LVHW010544100826
845148LV00013B/2597

* 9 7 8 1 7 8 3 6 4 4 5 6 8 *